Angels, Miracles
And the Kingdom

Written by Betsy O'Neal-Holt, PhD

Available at:
amazon.com/author/betsyholt
(use lowercase letters)

Copyright 2020, Betsy O'Neal-Holt, PhD
All rights reserved

DEDICATION

I dedicate this book and my devotion to the people who have enriched my life and gave me guidance, love and support in a way words cannot describe; my family and my daughter Kimberly Self Probus, DNP who continues to inspire me daily.

PREFACE

~ 3 ~

IN THE BEGINNING

My roots started in Florida and reborn in Fairbanks, Alaska. When asked what we are, we simply reply "We are believers." I think that sums it up well. Our roots go back over 60 years. It all started with The Ruskin Tabernacle and then The Evangelic House of Prayer. This is where the "Shekinah glory" fell. The word Shekinah does not appear in the Bible, but the concept certainly does.

The Jewish Rabbis coined this extra-biblical expression, a form of a Hebrew word that means "He caused to dwell". This signifies that it was a divine visitation of the presence or dwelling of the Lord God on earth. The Shekinah was first evident when the Israelites set out from Succoth in the escape from Egypt.

After leaving Succoth, they camped at Etham on the edge of the desert. By day the Lord went ahead of them in a pillar cloud to guide them on their way. By night He went before them in a pillar of fire to give them light, so they could travel by day or night. Neither the pillar cloud by day nor the pillar of fire by night left its place in front of the people. **Exodus 13:20-22, "And they took their journey from Succoth, and encamped in Etham, in the edge of the wilderness. And the Lord went before them by day in a pillar of a cloud, to lead them the way; and by night in a pillar of fire, to give them light; to go by day and night. He took not away the pillar of cloud by day, nor the pillar of fire by night, from before the people.**

These two churches are our root churches. This is where I first experienced true holy divine miracles, such as broken bones instantly healed, cancer healed and even the dead brought back to life. My father, Rev. Ervin O'Neal was the pastor of the House of Prayer for almost 40 years. It was he who prayed the prayer of faith for a child that was brought back to life. That story will be told later on.

Hebrews 13:8 says, "Jesus Christ the same yesterday, and today and forever". The things Christ and the Holy Spirit did for our forefathers He will certainly do for us according to **Hebrews 13:8.** I stand on that word and I not only believe it but I know it to be the true word of God. I claim the same Shekinah Glory for what He did before. He will do now and I claim the same victory and glory in His name and for His Kingdom.

This book is to help and assist you in understanding Kingdom living. Who are you in the Kingdom? Who is with you when you walk in the Spirit? Kingdom living is unlike any other life that you have ever experienced. Your responsibility is to bring the kingdom of heaven to earth.

What is the Kingdom? Where is the Kingdom? How do you know when you are in the Kingdom? What are your rights, benefits and responsibilities of being a child of God in his Kingdom? Most people do not understand what the Kingdom is nor do they understand the war that is going on in and out of the Kingdom. Through the reading of this book, you will obtain a clear understanding of not only who you are, but who is in you.

Our mission is simply to lead the way to a Kingdom life. Make no mistake, life is a battle between God and Satan and we are in an active war zone. This is a spiritual war but it spills over into the physical in the form of sickness, disease un-forgiveness, depression, drugs, alcoholism, and the likes. We must understand we are at war and what we must do to obtain the victory. The victory has already been won for us through Christ so we may walk and live in our inheritance. We must know and understand the weapons of the devil and what their purposes are. Are you prepared? Are you protected? We are here to help you. We never leave an injured soldier behind. We are first in on the battlefield and the last out. Our daily prayer should be, "Holt Spirit, Here I am, prepare, equip and send me."

Ephesians 6:12 "For we wrestle not against flesh and blood, but against principalities, against powers, against the rulers of the darkness of this world, against spiritual wickedness in high places".

Purpose of Life

Every human who is or has ever been born has a purpose in life or a reason for being here. In my mind, I see many, many souls in heaven. The Bible says He knew us before we were knitted in our mother's womb. So we had to be somewhere with God, in His presence, and in His kingdom. I think sometimes about what made God look out over all the souls and what made him pick you? Why did He pick you instead of the one right beside you? Did you have a bigger smile? Did your eyes sparkle brighter? Did you sing sweeter? Did you praise Him with more glory? Or perhaps He knew the task or the purpose you were being sent to do and thought, nobody could do it as well as you could.

So from Adam, all the way down the line to whomever the last person is to ever be born, you are hand-selected for a purpose. You may have a God-given talent that no one else has. You are given that talent for the glory of God. If you don't use the talent He gave you for His glory, He may take it back and give it to someone else. It's up to you to search and find out what that purpose is. Some people have more than one purpose in life.

My dad had a riddle and it was a good one. Who was the oldest man that ever lived and yet he died before his father? You would think that he couldn't be the oldest man that ever lived if his father died after he did. Think about that for a moment. Give up? The answer is Methuselah was the oldest man that ever lived and yet he died before his father because his father was Enoch. Enoch never died. He was translated! Translated means, move from one place or condition to another. Methuselah was 969 years old when he died. According to the book of Genesis, he was the father of Lamech and the grandfather of Noah. He is also mentioned in, 1st Chronicles and the Gospel of Luke.

So we all have a purpose or many purposes in life. Let's take a look here at Methuselah. He may have had several purposes in life but certainly the last purpose was to help Noah, his grandson, build the ark and he was 969 years old when the Ark was finished. Though some may mistakenly think Methuselah died in the flood, this is highly unlikely for several reasons. First, the Bible does not say he died in the flood. Just because he was not on the Ark does not mean he died in the flood. The flood was for the evil and rebellious people. Methuselah was neither. He did not deserve the punishment of the evil people. God is a just God and does not punish good people.

Methuselah was the child of a very godly parent. Enoch walked with God and had an extraordinary relationship with God. God would honor Enoch and Methuselah for their faithfulness and service to the kingdom. In those days, there was a seven day mourning period for the people who died. God's instruction for Noah and his family was to enter the Ark seven days in advance of the flood and that was for a few reasons. It is agreed by just about all theologians that Methuselah died immediately after the completion of the Ark. Noah and his family were on the Ark before the rains began and the flood came in observance of Methuselah's death. God said because of you, you and your whole household shall be saved. It is believed God spared Methuselah also because of his love for Enoch.

I hope that you spend time and study and research the facts. The point is, we all have a purpose. It may take some of us a short time and some of us 969 years to figure it out. What is my purpose? That is the question! When you know your purpose or your calling, you can move forward to accomplish what God has in store for you. One of our purposes is certainly to commune with God. To Praise Him, Worship Him, talk with Him and build a relationship with Him. We should do everything to glorify God. We are to live in God's purpose. God is God and He works all things, including your life, according to his purposes. **Psalm 57:2 "I cry out to God Most High, to God who fulfills his purpose for me."**

The ultimate purpose of life is peace in God's will and you because only a peaceful mind and heart can be full of love and compassion. Robert Bryne once observed, "The purpose of life is a life of purpose." To get anywhere, you need to define your end goal and the sooner you define it, the clearer everything else will become. A life without a purpose is a life without a destination. Purpose gives us direction and motivates us.

As I said before, the way you pray is very important. Seek Christ and purpose for your life. Begin to communicate with Christ. Talk with him and draw close to Him and see the many blessings and benefits He has to offer you. I learned a valuable lesson about talking to the Lord... that is He talks back. If you do not talk to Him directly how will you ever hear from Him? Talking is one thing...hearing is another. There is no such thing as a one-sided relationship, it take two.

I was a supervisor on the third floor of a large medical facility in Lakeland Florida. I had a routine when I got off work every day. I went home and changed clothes and walked around a small lake. This one particular day as I entered my home to change clothes, the phone began to ring. It was my mother! She was calling to tell me my uncle, who was her brother, was in the hospital because he had a serious stroke. She told his son she would call all her children (there are 5 of us) and tell us all to pray at exactly 6 pm for my uncle. As I began to walk around the lake I looked at my watch, it was 5:50 and I thought No, not yet. Not time to pray yet. I was meditating on the situation and the word of God but was not praying yet. When I looked at my watch again it was 6:00 on the dot. I began at that moment to pray. I knew all my family was beginning to pray also.

I was praying out loud, my arms were waving in the air. I probably looked like I was trying to land an airplane. I could feel the Spirit moving in the situation. I continued to pray and walk. When I was about to finish praying I said, "God I'm asking you for a sign that you are touching my uncle. I'm asking for a sign that you heard our prayers." At that exact moment, another jogger came around me and cut in front of me. All I could see was the back of his tee-shirt and there it was. There it was right on the back of his shirt, the sign I had asked for from God. The back of his shirt said, **"BY HIS STRIPES WE ARE HEALED"**. **Isa 53:5, But He was wounded for our transgressions; He was bruised for our iniquities: the chastisement of our peace was upon him; and with his stripes we are healed.**

Well, I shifted into high gear praising the Lord. I began to cry and thank him for the sign. I said out loud, "Lord I thank you for the sign you sent me. I know there is nothing greater than knowing the Almighty God hears us when we pray". Over and over again I said out loud, "There is nothing greater than knowing you hear us when we pray". Then the Lord spoke out loud to me and he said, "THERE IS ONE THING GREATER". I gasped for air. His voice and what he said just about took my breath away. I stopped walking and I stood under a tree and I said, "My Lord, how can that be? What could possibly be greater than knowing you hear me when I pray?" The Lord spoke again and said, "THE GREATER THING IS, THAT I ANSWER WHEN YOU PRAY". Well glory to God in the highest. He is right again. The greater thing is, knowing that he will answer when we call upon him. There is no other feeling like this.

I could not wait to get home and I ran the rest of the way. As soon as I raced in the door the phone was ringing again, and again it was my mother. I said, "Mom I've got to tell you something!!!" She said "No, I've got to tell you something." I replied but this is important, and she said "This is too and since I called you I talk first." I agreed and she began to tell me that my cousin just called her. He said my uncle was healed. The doctors had no idea what happened but they couldn't find anything wrong and he was being discharged and he was going home in a few minutes. **THAT'S MY KING!!!!**

Can we give the Lord a victory shout right about now? God is good and he is good all the time. When something happens and you can't explain it, it's a miracle. God is still on the throne and he knows what we need and when we need it. We just have to be living where we need to be living and ask him. After all, he does hear us when we pray and he will answer us.

The way you pray is very important and I can't express that enough. Our family came together in one mind, and in one accord, touching one thing (my uncle) and the Lord heard our prayers. Praying together is powerful. **Matthew 18:19 "Again, I say unto you, that if two of you shall agree on earth as touching one thing that they shall ask, it shall be done for them of my Father which is in heaven."**

Some people are called to teach the word of God, some are called to preach, some are called to be evangelist, some are called to be missionaries, some are called to be singers and some are called to be prayer warriors but no one is called to do nothing. Make no mistake about it… if you are on this earth, you are called to do something. Being a prayer warrior is very important. You may be called to spiritual battle at any moment. You need to be ready and prepared. But there is nothing to fear because the Lord said he would go before us into every battle. **Deuteronomy 31:8 "The Lord is the one who goes ahead of you, He will be with you. He will not fail** you or forsake you. Do not fear or be dismayed."

~ 19 ~

Fear Not

When I lived in Florida we had a gospel singing group called "Freedom". We performed at events and the Florida State Fair. One of the songs we sang was called "Fear Not." Before that song, I would always say there are 365 times in the Bible that we are told to fear not or be not afraid and there is 365 days in the year. This means that with the beginning of each and every day, we have a brand new promise that we have nothing to fear. That is so true. Yet life has a way of throwing things in our path that causes fear. We have to remember two things, First, He goes before us and second, there is nothing to fear. There is nothing to fear because there is no fear in the kingdom.

The war rages on between heaven and hell and prayer warriors fight many hard battles. They are usually the first ones in battle and the last ones out. No one is ever left behind, God loves us all. In my home I have a dedicated room called "The War Room". Here is where I spend many, many hours. When a serious prayer request comes in, I head to the War Room. There was a prayer request, so there is a battle to be won.

In that room, there is a large wooden cross. All prayer requests received are anointed and prayed over and attached to the cross. We pray over the cross and prayer requests every day. The cross also has pictures on it. Sometimes people send or bring pictures of other people. This is very specific and it is part of the prayer request so those pictures also are attached to the cross. The War Room is where I spend many nights. Sometimes I pray all day and all night. I also have my piano in there. That is where I write gospel songs and books.

When I'm deep in prayer and praying in the Spirit, I walk around in circles and pray out loud. One day I was doing this as I prayed and after about three hours I stopped and looked down. There in the middle of the room was my little Yorkie named Honey Bella. She was lying on her back and was asleep. I thought oh how cute is that? When I told my daughter Kimberly about it, she said, "When my momma prays even the dog gets slain in the Spirit." That was just a little humor there. Slain in the spirit is the term used for when the power of God comes on you so strong that you can no longer stand. The point is the War Room is where many serious hours are spent in serious prayer. Everyone should have a prayer room or a prayer closet.

I have a friend whom we will call Linda. She lived in Florida as I did then. She had been going through several hard battles. Her husband left for another woman and her son was on drugs. Her routine yearly physical revealed she had cancer. Her life was falling apart. She didn't know what to do or how to do it. She felt she could not handle it any longer. She called me and told me she was going to commit suicide. She said she had a loaded gun and she was going to use it as soon as she asked me for prayer and hoped God would forgive her for what she was about to do. I talked and prayed hard for her and I asked God to send her an angel to bring peace. We hung up the phone and I continued to pray and pray hard for her. After several minutes the phone rang and it was Linda again.

She said "something happened"! Something happened that was going to be hard to explain. She said "You know how it is when you are in a dark room with your eyes closed and someone walks in and turns the light on? You don't see the light because your eyes are closed but you see the brilliance from the light as it shines through your eyelids". Well, that was what she saw. At first, she wasn't sure if she should open her eyes or not. Then she slowly began to open them and started looking at the floor and then her eyes began to move upward. There standing in front of her was a very tall angel. He had a shield in one hand and a sword in the other hand. It was not like you would expect… You would think this is an angel of God and everything would be all shiny and golden. But it was not that way. His shield was tarnished and looked like it had dried blood on it. There were scratches and dents in his shield and looked as if it had been through many battles. When her eyes met his…he spoke to her and said, "I AM A WAR ANGEL…I COME TO WAR FOR YOU." At that moment she fell on her knees and began to thank God and praise Him for sending the help she needed. **That's my King who did**

that. No power in the universe can match His great power or His great love. **THAT'S MY KING!!!**

About 2 weeks went by and Linda called again. She said her husband asked her to forgive him and he came home and her son was in rehab. During her follow up visit at the doctor, she was told all the tests came back negative. I can't explain it other than believing when God does something, it is done completely and everything is made whole again. Never, underestimate the power and love of God.

We are overcomers by the word of our testimony. We are required to tell it when something powerful happens. If you have a miracle and you fail to tell it you may very well lose your miracle. There was a man who went to Sister Sykes's church (The Ruskin Tabernacle) who worked at a large facility in Tampa, Florida. He was injured and was told he would never walk again. After a long time, he decided to go to the Ruskin Tabernacle and ask Rev. Sykes to pray for him. She prayed the prayer of faith over him and immediately he received his healing and began to walk again. He was leaping for joy and was so excited. The following Monday he returned to work. As he walked past the security guard gate the guard on duty recognized him. The guard was excited to see him and so he called out, "Hey what happened to you? The man replied, "Oh nothing." At that very moment, he fell and never walked again.

We are overcomers by the word of our testimony. In other words, there is a price we have to pay for our healing. The price is to tell others what God has done for you and praise Him for it. If we fail on our part, how can we expect God to hold up his end of the contract? Healing is a benefit we have as Christians and believers of God.

Exercise your faith and belief. Practice your praise and sing of His goodness and mercy all the days of your life.

Amazing Things
God Will Show You

It is amazing the things God will show you if you are living in His kingdom. I was working and living in West Palm Beach, Florida. I drove home every Friday after work so I could go to church with my family. That is 202-mile drive one way. I didn't feel that was too far since I believe you have to worship where you get your needs met and your soul fed.

I was headed to Dade City, Florida to my dad's church. I was praying out loud and just having a regular conversation with the Lord. When I said, "Lord It's been a little while since I've heard from you and I need to hear from you today. So please show me something. I'm not asking for anything particular, I'm asking you to pick something and show me you are still with me." I drove another 50 miles or so just praying this kind of prayer.

I had pulled up to a stoplight on Memorial Blvd in Lakeland, Florida and all of a sudden my car began to rock back and forth. Even though my windows were rolled up and I had the air conditioner on, the wind began to blow. The wind was blowing inside my car so hard it was causing my car to rock back and forth. I looked around to see if any other drivers were looking and wondered what they were seeing. Here inside my car the warm winds were blowing and blowing hard. I could hear the sound of a mighty rushing wind. The wind blew so hard it blew one of my pearl earrings completely out of my ear and it was never found.

Then the Lord showed me the hollow of His hand and what and who was in there. I was in such awe of the Lord that I could not move. I could not drive when the light turned green. Amazing enough no one honked their horn at me. It felt like I was suspended in time. As I looked inside the hollow of His hand I saw golden lights beaming down and there were people I knew. Lots of people I recognized. One of the people was a high school friend named Kathysue Speer that I was very fond of in school but had lost contact with for years. Another person was my second cousin Sammy Brown-Taylor whom I had not seen since she was five. I was so happy to see them. It was almost a homecoming. I had a very calm and peaceful feeling, one of happiness and joy. I felt the presence of the Lord. I knew where I was and gazing inside, I could not take my eyes away. It was a place I didn't want to leave. But after a few moments, all of a sudden it was all over. I began to thank the Lord for showing me and giving me something of His choosing.

When we become children of the most-high God we come to a place where our belief and relationship with Him is unquestionable. If you are ever in doubt all you have to do is ask Him for a sign. It's all part of being in the kingdom of God. We are nothing without God, but with God we are everything. **Mark 16:17 "And these signs shall follow them that believe…"** When we are the believers and we diligently seek Him, He will show us signs. When we are part of the kingdom we are the believers.

What Is the Kingdom?

When we talk about the Kingdom of God we are talking about the rulership of a place. If you look up the word Kingdom in the Webster Dictionary you will find the definition states: The eternal kingship of God; The realm in which God's will is fulfilled; the reign or authority of God. Our walk through this life is moving toward heaven by way of the Kingdom. This is to say, moving in God's will and through His authority by His Spirit. At the end of all things, God's will, will be done!!!

When Jesus came, he came to restore dominion and return the kingdom of His Father to earth. Dominion means power, authority, jurisdiction, control, command, the right to govern, rule or determine. God created the earth and then the Garden of Eden; He then created Adam or man. He gave Adam dominion over the earth and dominion over all the animals of the earth. **Genesis 1:26... "And God said, Let us make man in our image, after our likeness and let them have dominion over the fish of the sea, and over the fowl of the air and the cattle and over all the earth and over every creeping thing that creepeth upon the earth."**

When Jesus came to earth, He taught by using parables or illustrations. The multitudes and sometimes the disciples did not understand at first. **St. Matthew 13:45..."The kingdom of heaven is like unto a merchant man, seeking goodly pearls; Who, when he had found one pearl of great price, went and sold all that he had and bought the land".** Are we willing to give up all that we have like the man who found a valuable pearl and go follow Christ? Or, like the man Jesus told to give away all that he had and give it to the poor and follow Him? **Mat 19:21 "Jesus said unto him, If thou will be perfect, go and sell that**

thou hast, and give to the poor, and thou shalt have treasure in heaven: and come and follow me.” We must be willing to do that very same thing although it may not be required of us. But we must be willing to put Christ first in our lives and follow His teaching and directions.

When you look at the kingdoms of the world, they promise you, health, wealth, love and joy. But all you see is unrest without peace and it offers deception because it gives death, sickness, greed and disease. Then you know this is not the kingdom of God. God's kingdom will provide blessings and all good things according to the following two Bible verses. **3 John 2, “Beloved, I wish above all things that thou mayest prosper and be in health, even as thy soul prospereth.” Luke 12:32 “Fear not, little flock; for it is your Father's good pleasure to give you the kingdom.”**

Where do we fit in the kingdom's life? We are the kingdom. Christ lives through us and us through him. If we serve God and believe His word then we are kingdom people. We do not walk around saying to everyone we meet that we are kingdom people, because God is not a respecter of persons. We do not have a title such as the president of the kingdom, bishop of the kingdom or ambassador of the kingdom. We know within the Holy Spirit that we are in fact, kingdom people. We walk differently, we talk and sound different and we live differently. We don't need to broadcast that because that would become pride. There is no room in the Kingdom for pride. **Proverbs 16:18 and 19; "Pride goeth before destruction and a haughty spirit before a fall. A man's pride shall bring him low, but honor shall uphold the humble in spirit."**

When pride comes, disgrace follows, but with humility comes wisdom. We need to get and keep a humble spirit. What is pride? It is being vain conceited, having vanity, ego, self-love, self-importance, self-exaltation, complacency or in other words having a big head. We have to learn and remember we are nothing without Christ. He is everything, He is all, and He is the Alpha and the Omega, the beginning and the end. He is the creator and without Him was nothing created.

Rev.1:8 "I am Alpha and Omega, the beginning and the ending, saith the Lord. Which is and which was and which is to come, the Almighty."

When we become part of the kingdom we are untouchable. In the world's way, when someone has a title of ambassador you just know you don't challenge that person. That title allows them to become the country they represent. If you put your hands on that person, then you do not just put your hands on a person. You are putting your hands on a country because they represent a country. We represent the kingdom of God and must govern ourselves according to the written word and must be led by the Holy Spirit. No man is allowed to walk up to you and put his hands on you without waking up the armies of God. Just because you have a title does not necessarily mean you are better than the next person. The Bible says God is not a respecter of persons.

That reminds me of a story my dad told in one of his sermons about a missionary who served God all his life in a foreign land. When the missionary became old he decided to return home. While on the long train ride to his home, he noticed there was an ambassador from another country on the same train. The ambassador was being treated like royalty with many people running around waiting on him hand and foot. When the train finally pulled into the station there on the station platform were just about all the town's people who turned out to welcome the ambassador. There was a band playing and the singers were singing and balloons flying in the air. Oh, what a welcome homecoming celebration it was. When the missionary got off the train there was no one to greet him. He slowly walked down the station's platform with tears in his eyes and He said, "Father, how can this be that all these people turned out to welcome the ambassador home and I have spent all my life serving in the missionary field and nobody is here to greet me and welcome me home?" The Lord spoke and said, "But my son, you are not home yet." So I ask you now, do you know who you are? Do you know how to get home? We are all just walking each other home but how we walk, is important.

That's a great story to remind us of who we are. Do you know who you are? Our rewards are not of this world but being held for us when we get home. God loves each of us dearly and He does not favor one over the other. What He has done for one, He will do for you. Many times when I pray I remind God that the scripture says, He is the same yesterday, today and forever. He changes not! So I remind Him what He did for Abraham, Isaac, and Jacob I expect Him to do for me because He is not a respecter of persons. **Romans 2:11, "For there is no respect of persons with God".**

The way you pray is very important. Say what you mean and mean what you say. Many, many years ago God made a covenant with Abraham and his descendants. I remind God that I am a direct descendant of Abraham's seed. I am the daughter of Abraham and I am part of the covenant. I am included in the contract. I know what the word says and I expect the word to work and become alive within me. I'm not a proud person. I'm not bragging on myself by saying that. I'm simply stating what God already knows and what He has already said. I am also the daughter of the King, the most-high God, the Lord of Lord and the love of my life. He wants His children to know who you are and where you come from and know the power that is within you. Your power is not of you and not of this world but comes from the Holy Spirit. The prayer that I sing daily, is a song called..."Come Breath upon Me Breath of God." Come breathe upon me and breathe upon our nation and upon the leaders of our nation. Breathe upon the children of the most high God with your love, mercy and grace. Lead us Holy Spirit to allow us to fulfill the calling and lead others. Yes, the way we pray and the words we speak are very important. Many times when I'm praying for healing I pray that the body comes in aliment with the word of God and the body must obey.

Some years ago we had a lady and her family who attended our church. She had a little three-year-old girl. We will call her Amy. One day the mother was washing clothes on the back porch and had a big tub of water there. After a while, the mom went into the house to take a break. Several minutes went by and the mom asked the other children where Amy was? Nobody knew. She became frantic and yelled, "everybody, look for Amy." The mother found little Amy floating in that big tub of water. She grabbed the child and ran toward the car. She screamed back over her shoulder and said, "Somebody call Brother O'Neal." (That was my dad. He was our pastor for almost 40 years). I heard the phone ring and I heard my dad say when? Where? I'm on my way. I threw on my shoes and headed for the door. I went with my dad and drove him most places. We arrived at the emergency room and the nurse at the desk asked if she could help us. My dad told her who we were there to see. She replied, "I'm sorry pastor you're too late. The child arrived DOA (Dead on Arrival)".

My dad said "I am not only a close friend of the family but I am their pastor and I have a legal right to see that baby". The nurse said "ok" and led us down a long hallway. At the end of the hallway, was a room on our right. We walked in and the nurse turned on the light and there was a curtain pulled around a stretcher. Lying there was a motionless little body, covered up on the stretcher. My dad pulled the sheet back and anointed Amy with oil and said, "I anoint you in the name of the Father, the Son and the Holy Ghost and you will live and you shall not die." At that moment Amy opened her eyes and took a deep breath. Amy is alive today and doing well. Can you give a victory shout of praise to God right now? **That's My King!!!**

The words he spoke were spoken with authority and full of faith. He spoke believing God's words are true and powerful. What God does for one He will do for another! There is no magic here. But there is a secret. The secret is you must be living a life that is close to God. You must have a close relationship with Him. You must be like Abraham and have a covenant with the Father.

Many people would like to have that kind of relationship and it is certainly possible, but to whom much is given, much is required. Most often people are not willing to pay the price for such a relationship. **Luke 12:48...For unto whom-**

soever much is given of him shall be much required."

What does that mean? To whom much is given, much will be required? This statement means we will be held responsible for what we have. If we are blessed with talents, wealth, knowledge, and the power to call on the Father, it is expected that we use these to glorify God and help others. With that also comes a sincere walk and relationship with God. To build a relationship with God can take a lifetime and the good news is it's never too late to start building.

You may ask how I know about these things. I believe in God the Father, the Son, and the Holy Spirit, sometimes referred to as the Trinity. Although the word "Trinity" is not in the Bible, the meaning certainly is. I believe not from what I've been told or heard but from what I've seen with my own eyes. In the very beginning, there was a woman name Rev. Rosa Sykes, there is a picture of her and her family in the back of this book.

One night after Sunday services at the Ruskin Tabernacle (located in Ruskin, Florida) instead of going home to rest, she went into a Sunday school room to pray. There the Lord spoke to her and said: "In the morning go to the hospital in Bradenton, FL and go to the third floor and room 301 and pray for the lady in the first bed on the right".

Sister Sykes did not think the Lord meant to go home, go to bed and get up in the morning and go. She thought He meant continue to pray until morning and then go. So she prayed all night. At 6 am the next morning, she got up from praying and drove to Bradenton. When she entered the room the lady in the first bed was my grandmother Nina and she was dying. She was in a lot of pain and she was suffering. Her body was a bit swollen and her face was gray. Sister Sykes stepped up to her bedside and introduced herself and told her why she was there. She asked Nina, "How would you like to go home and cook supper for your family tonight"?

Nina had no idea what this stranger was talking about. She didn't know anything about divine healing. Why she never heard of such a thing!! All Nina knew was she was in great pain and she was dying. Nina thought this woman was some kind of a fruitcake. Nina replied and said, "Just go away and leave me alone". You would have had to have known Sister Sykes to be able to appreciate her response. In her rough voice from years of hard preaching she replied, "Oh No, I can't do that. God told me to come to pray for you and I have to do that."

Nina only knew how much pain she was in and thought if she let this stranger pray, then she would go away. So Nina said, "OK". Sister Sykes anointed her with oil and prayed the prayer of faith and immediately Nina sat up in bed and said get my clothes I'm going home.

Nina told her son to go get the family and tell them to come to eat dinner. At that time we were living about 50 or 60 miles away. My uncle drove up to our house to tell us to come to eat because their mom was home. My mother, Betty Jo looked out the window of the house and saw her brother driving up the long driveway. She thought he had come to tell her that her mother had died. She began to cry. He got out of the car and said, "Betty don't cry momma's not dead, she is home cooking supper and wants everybody to come to eat dinner." Wait!!... What? What happened? She asked. He told her he didn't know what happened, just come eat supper and she would tell us all about it. We jumped in the car and headed to grandma's house. What happened was that day the Lord showed up and healed my grandma. She lived for many years after that and Sunday always found the family at church. Years later she did finally pass away. She loved to crochet and everything was pink or had pink in it. When she died her rose garden had died also from lack of care. Early one morning my grandpa walked out on the front porch with his cup of coffee before he went to work. He stood there looking at the dead rose garden and thinking about grandma. He was heartbroken and missed her dearly. He looked up at the sky and said, "Lord if there is a Lord and if Nina went to heaven, please show me a sign so I'll know it's you and everything is ok".

The next morning early he went to the front porch with his cup of coffee. There in the middle of the rose garden that was brown and dead was one rosebush full of vivid roses. With beautiful, bright green leaves and wouldn't you just know it... the roses were big and bright pink. The Lord has His way of answering prayers. If you take the time to notice, he puts little extra touches here and there to bring extra joy and sparkle. **That's My King!!!**

Help In Times of Trouble

I had an occasion not long ago to drive from my home in Fairbanks, Alaska to Tampa, Florida. I was alone except for my little dogs, Honey Bella and Gracie. Gracie is a long-haired Chihuahua. I drove out of Alaska and was driving across the Yukon Territory into Canada. There were miles and miles and many more miles that I didn't even pass another car. I began to get a little fearful since I was alone out in the middle of nowhere. I called my cell phone service before I left home and asked to be put on the international calling plan so I would have cell service in the Yukon and Canada. That was all fine and good except when I got in the Yukon Territory there was no service what so ever.

I started to think about what would happen if I had a flat tire. Or what would happen if one of these bears or a moose ran out in front of me and I hit them? What would happen if I was in an accident and not able to call for help? Nobody would know where to look for me. Nobody knows where I am!! I'm lost in the middle of the Yukon and nobody knows where I am!! Panic and fear started to set in. After only a short few minutes I was in tears and beginning to think this trip was not a good idea. But it was too late to turn back now. That didn't help me much either.

I kept thinking I'm lost and nobody knows where I am. I was just about a basket case. I could not stop driving and I could not stop crying. So I did the only thing I knew to do. I started praying that God would send a guardian angel to protect me and look after me. I said, "God right now nobody knows where I'm at. I'm lost and if something happens nobody will know where to look for my body. I may never be found. I'm lost!!" I continued telling the Lord how lost I was. I kept trying to explain to Him so He would understand the situation I'm in. "Lord, I'm alone and I'm lost! Do you hear me? Do you understand me? I'm alone and I'm lost."

I was so caught up in my moments of fear and panic. I temporarily forgot the Lord knows all things. Just at that moment, I began to smell something. I was not sure what the scent was but it was getting stronger. The two little dogs began to run from one side of my vehicle to the other side and they were sniffing very loudly, so I knew whatever the smell was, they could smell it too. I'm not sure if I can describe the smell but it was a mixture of lavender and myrrh and something else but what was the other ingredient? I did not know. I could not put my finger on it but it was a sweet scent. At that moment the Lord spoke to me and said, "Betsy, you are not lost… I know where you are." A deep calmness came over me like a warm gentle hug. I instantly felt peace and security. When I could finally speak I said, "So this is the smell of the Lord!!" I was in the presence of the Lord. Then I felt a bit foolish for allowing myself to get so worked up. Yes indeed, He did know where I was all along and there was nothing to fear.

Sometimes it's the small miracles in our daily life that gets us through each day. It's the small things you see that are "faith builders." When we recognize the small miracles, they start quickly to stack up to the big ones. There are times when we have small miracles in our lives and we don't take notice of them. The small things sometimes are taken for granted. Every time we take a breath and there is no pain, it is a small miracle! There are millions of people in the world who have some form of pain, from a small amount to a major pain just staying alive. When we get in our cars and drive to the store or across the country and we are safe, it's a small miracle. There are millions of people who start-out every day and don't make it to their destination. We never know when our last moment on this earth will be. So it pays to be prepared just in case. All of our days are numbered.

I can't tell you how many times I lost my car keys or my wallet. I would say a little prayer, "Lord, right now you are the only one who knows where it is. Can you show me?" It's almost like magic...I usually walk right to it and say, "Oh, there you are! Thank you, Lord for showing me!" If you ask and believe, he will answer. Every person has already been given a measure of faith. **Romans 12:3 "For I say, through the grace given unto me, to every man that is among you, not to think of himself more highly than he ought to think, but to think soberly, according as God hath dealt to every man the measure of faith." Matthew 17:20 And Jesus said unto them, "Because** of your unbelief: for verily I say unto you, If ye have faith as a grain of mustard seed, ye shall say unto this mountain, Remove hence to yonder place; and it shall remove; and nothing shall be impossible unto you." Why did He use the mustard seed as an example? He used it because the mustard seed is very small. Yet it grows into something much larger than itself. We must look for the small miracles to grow our "faith seed" into something much larger as well. If we are not looking for the small miracles, we will not see them and our seed will not grow.

Every time you use your faith it gets stronger. The stronger your faith is, the stronger you become. Is your faith still the size of a mustard seed? The mustard seed is the smallest seeds. Yet just this small size can move mountains. Sometimes when I'm facing issues I know satan is sending those issues to cause me stress, I say, "Stand back satan, I have a mustard seed and I'm not afraid to use it." Small prayers produce small results. Pray big! Dream big! Praise big! Sing loud and give thanks! Hope big, because your hope is in Christ the Lord.

Another big faith movement was the day I was working and a friend named Randy came running in my store and he was shouting at me, telling me my brother just had an accident just down the road and his Jeep was turned over. I ran out, got into my car and started going that way. The whole time I was praying, "God don't let it be him. Please turn back the hand of time and don't let it be him."

As I approached the accident scene I could see the red jeep upside down. I saw the red and white scuba sticker on the bumper and my mind said it was him. In my heart, I kept saying "It is not him because the Lord has turned back the hands of time and I refuse to accept this." I walked up the side and the police officer said I could not go up there. I told him someone said it was my brother but I refuse to believe that. He asked my brother's name and I told him. He replied, "No ma'am, it's not him".

I cried the entire way back to work thanking God for His mercy and understanding and love. You may think, well that was not a powerful story because it was not your brother. I'm choosing to believe the Lord sent guardian angels to protect my brother and change the things that were into the thing that were not. This was a powerful blessing. We have the ability, to speak things that are not as thou they were. We have many blessings every day. We may not notice them but they are there. If you don't see blessings daily then you need to slow down and look for them. One small blessing will lead to another and then another. **Deuteronomy 28:2, "And all**

these blessings shall come on thee, and overtake thee, if thou shall hearken unto the voice of the Lord thy God."

Now, look at that first part of that scripture. Where it states, "All these blessing shall come on thee and overtake thee." In my mind, I see many of us running away. Running in the other direction we are not sure about this. What is a blessing? Do I want it? Do I need it? I see people running when all of a sudden a blessing sees you and runs after you, catching up to you little by little. You keep running and you keep looking back; you are getting out of breath. But you continue to run, and that blessing is slowly catching up little by little until the blessings of the Lord will run you down and then run over you as they overtake you. That is just a little funny thought. But you can't run from God. You can't run from the blessings of the Lord.

My brother, Larry picked up a hitchhiker once on his way home from work late one night. Once the stranger got in his car he started talking about the Lord. He kept on and on talking about things of the Lord. As Larry exited the interstate, he apologized to the man. He said, "I am sorry but this is my exit." The man said that it was ok and thanked him for the ride. As Larry was about to pull back onto the road he looked to wave goodbye to the stranger and he was gone. Larry looked up and down the highway but he was nowhere to be found.

Many angels are unaware at the moment. But something is always done or said to let you know who they are and that they were sent to you. These are messengers from the most-high God. They are sent to give you a message. Beware of your surroundings. Get prayed up and stay that way. Be ready instantly in season and out of season. You may never know when a message is being sent to you and you don't want to miss it. Here is a little side note....Be very careful who you disrespect, disregard, dismiss, or dishonor in the flesh because you have no insight of their rank in the Spirit.

I attended Bible school in Lakeland Florida. It was owned and operated at the time by Rev. and Mrs. Meyers. Times were hard back then and money was hard to come by. One day Brother Meyers was sitting on his porch and a stranger was walking down the dirt road. There were not many houses on that road. Brother Myers wondered where the stranger was going. The man walked up to the front porch and asked Brother Myers for change, to buy a cup of coffee. Brother Myers thought I only have a 50 cent piece in my pocket and I can't help him. So he told the stranger that he didn't have the money to spare. He said if you walk on down the road about a mile there is a big house on the left and I'm sure they can help you. The stranger replied, "I wasn't sent to them, I was sent to you." And with that the stranger walked off.

A few seconds later it hit Brother Myers what the stranger said, "I wasn't sent to them, I was sent to you". Brother Myers jumped off the porch and ran after the stranger; he called after him but could not find him. Brother Myers missed a blessing that day because he was not prepared for a stranger to pass by. Make sure you are prepared so you don't miss a blessing. We encounter angels unaware and messages every day.

Hand Writing On the Wall

Let's take a look at the story about the handwriting on the wall. You can find this story in Daniel chapter 5. In summary, King Belshazzar was believed once to be the son of Nebuchadnezzar, the Babylonian inscriptions indicate that he was, in fact, the eldest son of Nabonidus, who was king of Babylon from 539 to 555.

The story states King Belshazzar had looted the first temple in Jerusalem during its destruction. King Belshazzar holds a great feast and he drinks from the vessels that had been looted. Belshazzar had likewise blasphemed God and so God sent a hand to write a message on the wall for the King. The King did not know what the message said. He called his wise men to tell him what it said and what it meant but they had no idea what the message said. Then someone said the king should send for Daniel, as he was a man of God and certainly he would be able to read it. When Daniel arrived he looked at the writing on the wall. It said, "Mene, Mene, Tekel, Upharsin," This is of Aramaic origin. Daniel interpreted it to mean that God had doomed Belshazzar's kingdom.

Today the handwriting on the wall is there for many of us, and many times. But it comes in three parts. First, you have to be aware and notice that there is in-fact a message for you. Second, you have to be able to read it or interrupt it.
Third, you have to know how to apply the message to your life. This is important. If you are not living in a relationship with the Lord, how will you know when you see a sign? How will you know what it says or what it means? Many times you will just stroll on down life's path and miss it. My mother used to say, Stay in touch with heaven and stay in tune with the Lord. Build

your relationship with God. The adventures ahead will be amazing.

I have a story that is close to my heart. My grandson, whom we will call Garrett, was about 3 years old. He was having a very hard time in life. His parents had divorced and they had shared custody. Every other week he spent with his mom. He was having issues adjusting to the lifestyle and having step-parents in his life. He cried every time he was put to bed. The door was closed, the light turned off and he was alone. One day my daughter came into my mother's house, where I was visiting, and said it broke her heart to leave him but there was nothing she could do about it. My mother said we need to pray for Garrett right now. My daughter, my mother and I formed a prayer circle in the kitchen and we all began to pray and call out to God on Garrett's behalf, asking God to help. I could hear my mother in my left ear praying and she was saying, "Lord, please send an angel to Garrett. Let him see and feel the touch of the angel and give him peace and comfort." So I began to agree and pray the same way. After a moment we were all praying the same thing. We were all praying in one mind and in one accord for the same thing.

The following week when my daughter went to pick him up from his dad's house, the dad asked her, "Who do you know named Thomas?" My daughter replied and said she didn't know anyone named Thomas. He then asked, "Well who does your mother know named Thomas?" She again replied no one that I know of. He began to tell the story that Garrett no longer cried when he was put to bed. Instead, he would look over in the corner and tell his dad, "Look, there is Thomas again." I believe that the Lord did just what we asked Him to do. He sent an angel named Thomas to comfort and bring peace to Garrett.

A couple of weeks went by and I had Garrett once again at my mother's house. When it was time to take him home, I asked my mom if she would like to go with me and of course, she did. Once we entered the neighborhood I started to slow down a bit. I looked to my left and on a little hill was a house with two children in the front yard. There was a little girl who looked to be about 7 years old and a little boy who looked to be about 5. As I was slowing down the little boy lost his ball and it rolled out of the yard and right in my lane of traffic. The little boy followed, as he ran after the ball. I slammed on brakes and my tires began to screech and smoke. All of a sudden everything started moving in super slow motion. I heard the sound as my car hit the little boy. What a terrible thud sound. I saw the little boy roll around the front of my car and down the driver's side. I saw his face out my driver's window. Then he disappeared for a brief moment. I said to my mother, "Did I hit him?" She did not answer. She was leaning forward gripping the dash with both hands. I screamed, "DID I HIT HIM?" She replied, "I don't know."

I looked around and didn't see the child. I was afraid he was under my car. My heart was beating so hard I could feel it through my chest. My breath was rapid and I was crying as I got out of my car and on my knees to look under the car. But to my surprise, he was not under my car. Where could he be? Was he flipped over in the ditch? Was he somehow still in front of the car? I stood up and said, "Oh God please help me find him right now." I turned around in the same spot a couple of times looking up and down the street. Then all of a sudden I saw him. There he was, he was standing in his yard looking at me.

But...wait...What? What just happened? How could he be standing in his yard? I was in shock. I could not move for a few moments. I have no idea how long I stood in the road looking at him. Yes, yes there he was standing in his yard by his sister.

At that moment I returned to my car. I sat down behind the steering wheel and I wanted this moment to be remembered by Garrett for a long, long time. Here is a very important lesson I told Garrett. You never go in the road. If your ball rolls in the road, you always go get your mom or your dad. You never go in the road for any reason. That little boy could have died. I wanted Garrett to realize how important this lesson was. Garrett listened to me and then he spoke up and said, "But Grams, Thomas was in the road." Ok, well now I got the rest of the story. I shouted so loud and praised God. That makes perfect sense. If Thomas was sent to Garrett to protect him if he was in danger, Thomas would be there and there he was right in the middle of the road. Doing what God sent him to do. Protect and bring peace.

I know what I heard and I know what I saw and my mother was there as a witness to it all. What satan meant for evil, God turned around for good. God wins every time. Satan meant to cause destruction and evil and pain. But God intervened. The words we speak are important!! We have the power and ability to speak things that are not as though they were. That's my King!

The Seed

Romans 4:17 "it is written: I have made you a father of many nations." Abraham is our father in the sight of God. In whom he believed the God who gives life to the dead and calls into being things that were not. Speaking things into existence is another way of saying "let there be." God first did this in the book of Genesis, chapter one states: **"In the beginning God created the heaven and the earth. And the earth was without form, and void; and darkness was upon the face of the deep. And the Spirit of God moved upon the face of the waters."** And God said, "Let there be light and there was light. And God saw the light that it was good: and God divided the light from the darkness. And God called the light Day and the darkness he called night. And the evening and the morning were the first day. And God said, "Let there be a firmament in the midst of the waters and let it divide the waters from the waters. And God made the firmament and divided the waters which were under the firmament from the waters which were above the firmament and it was so. And God called the firmament Heaven. And the evening and the morning were the second day. And God said, Let the waters under the heaven be gathered together unto one place, and let the dry land appear, and it was so. And God called the dry land Earth, and the gathering together of the waters called the Seas; and God saw that it was good. And God said, Let the earth bring forth grass, the herb yielding seed and the fruit tree yielding fruit after his kind, whose seed is in itself, upon the earth and it was so. And the earth brought forth grass and herb yielding seed after his kind and the tree yielding fruit, whose seed was in itself and his kind and God saw that it was good. And the evening and the morning were the third day. And God said,

"Let there be lights in the firmament of the heaven to divide the day from the night, and let them be for signs and for seasons, and for days and years. And let them be for light in the firmament of the heaven to give light on the earth and it was so. And God made two great lights, the greater light to rule the day and the lesser light to rule the night, he made the stars also. And God set them in the firmament of the heaven to give light upon the earth. And to rule over the day and over the night, and to divide the light from the darkness and God saw that it was good. And the evening and the morning were the fourth day. And God said, "Let the waters bring forth abundantly the moving creature that life, and fowl that may fly above the earth in the open firmament of heaven. And God created great whales, and every living creature that moveth, which the waters brought forth abundantly, after their kind, and every winged fowl after his kind and

God saw that it was good. And God blessed them, saying Be fruitful and multiply and fill the waters in the seas and let fowl multiply in the earth. And the evening and the morning were the fifth day. And God said, Let the earth bring forth the living creature after his kind, cattle and creeping thing and beast of the earth after his kind and it was so. And God made the beast of the earth after his kind and cattle after their kind and everything that creepeth upon the earth after his kind and God saw that it was good. And God said, Let us make man in our image, after our likeness and let them have dominion over the fish of the sea, and over the fowl of the air and over the cattle and over all the earth and over every creeping thing that creepeth upon the earth. And God said, Let us make man in our image, after our likeness and let them have dominion over the fish of the sea and over the fowl of the air and over the cattle and over all the earth and over every creeping thing that creepeth upon the earth. So God created man in his own image, in the image of God created he him male and female created he them. And God blessed them and God said unto them, Be fruitful and multiply and replenish the earth and subdue it and have dominion over the fish of the sea and over the fowl of the air and over every living thing that moveth upon the earth. And God said Behold, I have given you every herb bearing seed, which is upon the face of all the earth and every tree in which is the fruit of a tree yielding seed, to you it shall be for meat. And to every beast of the earth and to every fowl of the air and to everything that creepeth upon the earth, wherein there is life. I have given every green herb for meat and it was so. And God saw everything that he had made and behold it was very good. And the evening and the morning were the sixth day."

So here you see how God spoke the words "Let there be" and so it was. You and I have the power through Christ to speak the words to create something that is not in existence and it shall come into existence. We can speak blessings and curses and when we pray we have the power and ability to speak healing and blessings through Christ.

Another thing to look at in this chapter, according to the creation of the third day… let's look at that part again. There is a wonderful message in there that most people miss. If you are looking at the third day in the KJV Bible, it should start about verse 11. **"And God said, Let the earth bring forth grass, the herb yielding seed, and the fruit tree yielding fruit after his kind, whose seed is in itself, upon the earth and it was so."** The seed came first and within that tiny seed was a big fruit tree. The seed has to die out to its self so the big fruit tree can grow. The big tree then yields fruit and the fruit yields yet more seeds to start the cycle all over again. So the tiny little seed had within itself all it needed. It contained everything it needed to produce good works such as the tree, then the fruit and then more seeds.

That's the way we are. From the time we were created and formed in our mother's womb we are equipped with everything we need. We must first die out to Christ and belong to Him not to ourselves. To die out to Christ means that we place Him and His will before our own. Our soul has everything within itself to fulfill our purpose in life and prosper and be in good health. Everything was created to have everything it needs within itself. Look at the fish... They swim because it was within them to swim. Birds fly because it was within them to fly. You have within you to be successful to grow, to be happy and most of all to serve God. It's already there so why not use it?

We may not always get what we want but we will always get what we need. Mat 6:33 "But seek ye first the kingdom of God, and his righteousness, and all these things shall be added unto you." Sometimes things happen and we wonder why. We don't understand it at that moment. But we trust in God and believe He sees and He knows what we need. We have to believe and know that He has our best interest at heart. Sometimes we may pray for a new house or a new car. God answers but it was not the answer we were expecting. He answered, "The one you have is good enough. You don't need a new one right now." Maybe we didn't get that house we wanted to buy. But later down the road, we find out there was a better house for us. Then we as humans understand what God had in His plans for us. That happened to me once. I wanted to build a new house and it seemed for whatever reason it was just not happening. About two months later I saw a blueprint of a better house and there was no issue in building that new house. God saw in my future and He knew a better house was coming. That first house was simply not mine. It is like peeling an onion. You peel off all the layers and what is left is yours.

That's the way it is with a lot of things in our life. That girlfriend or boyfriend we thought we loved so much but ended up marrying somebody else was in-fact not ours. God saw and He knew it or that job we wanted and didn't get was not meant for us. God saw ahead and He knew what was best for us. We have to put our trust in Him in all things and believe He is the creator and He knows what is best for us. The question becomes not why didn't I get what I wanted? But Lord, how can I trust you more? How can I praise you more? Lord please, help me find and fulfill my purpose in this life. Picture yourself as the tiny little seed, having within you all the things you need and all those things came from your heavenly Father. He had selected for just you, for such a time as you need them.

Speak To the Storm

One day my mother and father were home and my mom heard a loud noise that sounded like a freight train coming? She called out to my dad to see if he heard it also. He yelled back to her and told her to get on the floor there was a tornado coming. Instead of falling to the floor and looking for cover, my mother ran to the front door and opened it to lookout. Oh my heavenly God there it was. It was a tornado and it was across the highway and headed straight to their front door. My mother raised both her hands and she yelled at the storm and demanded that it cease.

The tornado kept coming right across the road. It was staring right in the face of my mom and attempting to make her afraid. She stood there with both arms raised in the air and kept speaking the word of God over that tornado. It moved fast and loud and continued to cross the road and into the front yard it came and bringing with it all the evil winds and force it had. Yet she stood there arms raised in the air. The tornado came almost up to the house, and then something strange happened….the tornado lifted off of the ground and went over their house and sat itself down in the back yard. Destruction was everywhere across the road from where it came and in the front yard….BUT…no harm came to them or their dwelling. According to Psalm 91, "No harm shall come near thee or thy dwelling…"

Let me explain a little bit of this. If you read **Exodus 17th** chapter you will find that Moses was in Rephidim and Moses told Joshua to pick out the men and they were to fight Amalek. He told Joshua tomorrow he would stand on top of the hill with the rod of God in his hand while the battle was going on. The next day Moses, Aaron, and Hur went up to the top of the hill. When

Moses held up his hands, Israel prevailed and when he let down his hands, Amalek prevailed. So while Moses held up his hands toward God they were winning. But after a bit, Moses' hands became very heavy and his arms grew tired and he let down his hands. Each time he did, the battle turned and Amalek began to win again. So Aaron and Hur held up his arms and hands, with one on each side of Moses until the sun went down. And the Lord said unto Moses, "Write this for a memorial in a book." And Moses built an altar and called the name of it "Jehovah Nissi."

You must understand that physical obedience brings Spiritual release and blessings. Today's victories were yesterday's battles. We are being called into battle every time we receive a prayer request. Every time we engage in battle over our marriage, over our finances, over our children, over our families, over sickness and death, praising God is a key factor. We have angels assigned to each of us to help us bring the blessings of the Lord and the things we truly need. So we should focus on praising him with all we have within us. David said, "Bless the Lord oh my soul and all that is within me." Who was David talking to here? He was talking to his soul. 100 million angels are praising God according to. **Revelations 5:11-12 "And I beheld and I heard the voice of many angels round about the throne and the beasts and the elders and the number of them was ten thousand times ten thousand, and thousands of thousands; Saying with a loud voice, Worthy is the Lamb that was slain to receive power and riches, and wisdom and strength and honor and glory and blessings."**

Angels Unaware

When I lived in Lake Wales, Florida I babysat for a little boy who we will call Clay. He was about 2 years old. Sometimes on Saturday his mom would call and say "He is crying out of control, could I come get him for a little while." So this one Saturday morning I went to pick him up. We went to a fast-food drive-in and then headed to the park. Once at the park, the place was full of people. Hundreds of people were everywhere. They were having a fall bazaar and white tents and tables were everywhere. We ate our lunch and walked over to sit in the swing. I had Clay on my lap, swinging slowly. Soon, an old man seemed to appear out of nowhere. He stood before me in a faded red plaid shirt that looked almost pink and a pair of overall's that had a rip in one knee. His skin was bronze as if he worked out in the sun all the time. He did not introduce himself. He just said, "There have been many people

I've tried to talk to today and nobody will listen to me." I felt kind of sorry for the ole gent and replied, "I'll listen." He sat down in the swing next to me and immediately began to talk about the end of the world. He spoke of what was going to happen and when. He told me of signs to look for and things to watch out for. He was talking so fast I had no time to respond. I just kept shaking my head in a positive motion and saying un-huh!

After a time all of a sudden he stopped talking. He looked at me and said there has always been something in the Bible that you wanted to know and could not find the answer to. Again, I shook my head yes. He went on to say "you want to know about Peter. Peter said I'm not worthy to be crucified as my Lord and he requested to be crucified upside-down." Again, I shook my head. It never occurred to me to think or ask, how do you know that? I know the scriptures tell us that part but do not say if that ever actually happened. Now here is this stranger telling me this story. After several long minutes of just looking at me, he finally replied, "HE WAS".

Then he went on talking about the end of the world as if he never paused to talk about Peter. When he finished talking he got up out of the swing, without another word, without a thank you for listening, without a goodbye or saying, "have a nice day." He simply walked across in front of me about 8 feet to the curb and he stopped. He turned around and looked at me for what seemed several minutes. My eyes were glued upon him. I could hear my heart beating. Finally, in a soft voice that I can still hear today, he spoke and said, "BETSY, IF YOU EVER NEED ME CALL ME." Then he turned around and with one step he stepped off the curb and into the street, then he disappeared right in front of my eyes.

There have been a few special times in my life where I felt like I was up against a stone wall. I could not get through, I could not get over or around and I said, "Lord, do you remember that day in the park? Well, I do. You said if I ever needed you to call you and I'm calling you now. Those times the Lord always, always answered my prayers. I do remember and Lord, help me to always remember and serve him.

The man in the park never introduced himself to me nor I to him. How did he know my name? Why did he choose to talk to me that day? We must be aware of our surroundings at all times for we might be entertaining an angel unaware. Pay attention, be on guard and be seeking the Lord. Go daily with praise on your lips and a song in your heart.

I am very careful about what I ask for and I'm careful about how often I ask. I saw a post online once that said, "Prayer over Fear." I have no idea who wrote that or who quoted it but it speaks truth. Prayer and praise build things and the first thing it builds is a bond and establishes a relationship and second, it builds faith. I believe to have a strong walk of faith and to build a good relationship you must give praise more than you ask for things. The Lord wants us to spend time with Him. A better way of saying that is the Lord wants to hear from us and not only when we are facing trouble or in need. Also, be aware your angels hear what you say and they respond accordingly. If you speak negative and doubt you will get what you speak. Make sure your words are of positive thoughts and blessings. What you sow you shall reap. Reap a good, positive harvest and good life.

My younger brother used to have a way he explained things. He would come to me and start to tell me a story or something that happened and it was usually a story that somehow he was involved in. He would always start with... "I was just minding my own business when...." He would tell the event with profound intensity and humor. It didn't take long before I knew, here comes a good story... I better listen up. He was a funny guy who always had something going on. I began to enjoy hearing his stories. They were funny and you laughed and truly enjoyed it.

That is the way the Lord is. He created Adam and Eve and He came in the cool of the day to commune with them. Commune means to converse, talk, often with profound intensity, intimate communication or rapport as sharing your heart and mind with God in prayer. God wanted to talk with Adam and Eve and He wanted to hear from them. The Lord wants to commune and talk with you as well. Taking the time to get to know Him is so easy. My mother said many times, "It is free yet it costs you everything." Meaning it does not cost you money, but it will cost you devotion, your time, your life serving him. Ask yourself the question... Am I ready for a relationship and to see the glory of the Lord?" Build your relationship with Christ as if He is your best friend. One who will help you during your worse times! One who can help you when no one else can! People let you down but Christ never will.

There was a time in my life when I owned and drove a semi-truck. I have a class A, CDL license so I would drive from Florida, where I lived, to the West Coast. Sometimes I drove as a team driver with my husband and sometimes I drove solo. One trip when I was driving solo I had a delivery appointment in California that was a bit tight. I drove and drove until I was very tired. I pulled into several rest areas only to find no parking place. The rest areas were full and trucks were parked on the ramp to get in or out of the rest area. I felt like my eyes were about to dangle off my chin. It felt as if I had sand in them.

I just didn't think I could make it to another rest area. I began to pray, "Lord help me make another mile. " I drove another one and then another one and another. Finally, about 5 am I found a rest area with a parking spot. I pulled in and I didn't think I was going to be able to get out of the driver's seat. I managed somehow to get in the bunk and fell across the bed. I could not even change my clothes. I was so tired I could not speak. I was weak and unsure of what was going to happen next. I was alone and could not help myself.

When you drive for a living, every mile brings unexpected things your way. It could be just an adventure or it could be a danger. I never, ever go to sleep without thanking the Lord for His mercy and guardian angels He sends for my protection. I ask for guardian angels to encamp round about me and this day was no exception. But how can I pray and thank Him when I am so exhausted I can't talk, can't sit up and can't reach for my Bible. I had to make contact with Him somehow. But how was I going to acknowledge Him in this state of weakness and exhaustion? Just before I fell into a deep sleep I raised one hand just a couple of inches and I waved at Him. I know He saw me and the condition I was in and I know He knew the condition of my heart and my efforts. I hope He chuckled a little bit and said something like… "That's my girl!"

I know and recognize that He is the Lord God Almighty. We should honor Him in all things. But He is also my very best friend. Sometimes I speak to Him as if he is just that...my best friend. He knows all my secrets, all my desires and all the hidden places in my heart. So I talk to Him and communicate as such. Of course, there are times I pray and times I praise. But having a relationship where you can talk as a friend to friend is very important and rare these days. Some people don't know you can have the Lord as your best friend. It depends on what you are willing to do to achieve that kind of relationship. There are also times in life when things happen so fast you need to touch heaven immediately. It is good to get prayed up and create that bond with Him because sometimes there is no time to get prepared to call on Him.

Sometimes God sends messenger angels. They come with a message from the

Lord. They can't carry on a conversation about this or that or worldly things. They come for a reason and a purpose. That purpose is, they have a message and it is for you. Sometimes it's not just a message. Sometimes there is something you need and they will bring it to you. They won't come to wash your car or take the trash out because you can do those things yourself. The Lord knows what you need and he will dispatch angels on an assignment to help you.

Angelos is the Greek word normally translated into English as "angel." Angelos means "one who brings a message." Much of what we know about God is revealed to us by God through His names. A few of the names that we know and are popular is as follows:

YHWH is pronounced Yahweh meaning the King of Kings

The Light meaning the Lord of Lords

The Great I AM meaning the Lord of Hosts
Christians refer to him as Ancient of Days
meaning Father
ABBA meaning Father God
Elohim meaning Most High
El-Shaddai meaning Yahweh-God Almighty
Jehovah meaning Adonai
Jehovah-Jirah meaning Jehovah Shammah

Let's look at a couple of these names. The name El-Shaddai appears in the Bible 48 times. Seven times as El-Shaddai and five of those times in Genesis, once in Exodus and one in Ezekiel. Biblical translations as well as other early translations usually translate El-Shaddai as "God Almighty." The Greek translation as seen in Psalm 91:1 is translated as "The God of heaven." El-Elyon na Adonai when all put together is a combination of meanings. "God Most High", "Please My Lord," "Na" is translated please or I beseech thee. Elyon is translated into English as "God Most High."   Jirah or

Jehovah, Jirah is certainly Greek words translated means "The Lord will provide." Such as when Moses was about to offer his son as a sacrifice and God provided a ram. Jehovah Nissi is a name meaning, "the Lord my banner."

The first scripture regarding El-Shaddai is found in **Genesis 17:1. "And when Abram was ninety years old and nine (99), the Lord appeared to Abram and said unto him, "I am the Almighty God; walk before me and be thou perfect." Exodus 6:2-3 "And God spake unto Moses and said unto him, I am the Lord, and I appeared unto Abraham, unto Isaac, and unto Jacob by the name God Almighty, but by my name JEHOVAH was I not known to them."**

God also gave names to His angels to reveal something about them. Only three angels are named in the Bible but the Bible gives us a look at those names in contrast with the name of Jesus. **"He shall save His people from their sins." Matthew 1:21** He (Jesus) hath by inheritance obtained a more excellent name than they, referring to the angels, as found in **Hebrew 1:14**.

Lucifer means; Bearer of Light

Gabriel means; Man of God

Michael means; Who is like the Lord

There are other names such as Gabriel and Raphael that are popular today. It is good to do a study of these names.

Lucifer was the original name for the devil or satan. This name does not refer to the current character of satan but his original created purpose. He originally possessed a high level in heaven according to Isaiah 14:14. He was cast down because of his desire to rise above God. His name means bearer of light, reflecting his purpose to bear the light of God. So Lucifer should have been a light bearer to Christ who is the true light that lights every man that comes.

Gabriel is the messenger angel of God. The name Gabriel means "man of God." His character trait is strength.

You can find scriptures relating to Gabriel in the following:

Daniel - 8:16, 9:21 and 28

Zacharias – Luke 1:11, 19

Mary- Luke 1:26, 27

Joseph–Matthew 1:20, Matthew 2:13, 19

Jesus in Gethsemane – Luke 22:43

The apostles in prison – Acts 5:19

Philip – Acts 8:26

Peter – Acts 12:7

Herod – Acts 12:23

Paul – Acts 27:23

John – Rev. 22:8

Michael is the most powerful angel. Michael is usually related to Israel and the resurrection according to **Daniel 10:13, 12:1, 2:1** and **Thess. 4:19**. In the **9th chapter of Jude** he is described as the archangel, which means he is highest in the order of angels. His name means "Who is like the Lord?" You can find scriptures relating to Michael in the following:

Daniel 10:13, 21; 12:1
Satan on earth – Jude 9
Satan in heaven – Rev 12:7

There are other types of angels and we will get into some of those later on. However, let's look at two of them now. They are angels that we are not given their names but rather the type of angels, Cherubim and Seraphim. The Cherubim are a group of angels that guard the holiness of God from man's sin. After Adam and Eve sinned, a cherub guarded the gate to Eden. Two of the likenesses of them were placed on the Ark of the Covenant in the tabernacle. **Exodus 25:18-22**, and also in the temple according to **Kings 6:23-29** indicate this. The statues stood symbolically in the protection of the presence of God himself.

Seraphim are a higher class of angel. The word "Seraphim" means "burners." Like the cherubim they are protectors of the holiness of God as found in **Isaiah 6:3**. So when the Seraphim cleansed Isaiah with live coals from the altar as stated in **Isaiah 6:6-7**, this order of angels are connected many times with sacrifice and cleansing. The Seraphim cry continually to each other, "Holy, Holy, Holy is YHWH of hosts; the whole earth is full of His glory." Seraphim with Cherubim are the heavenly creatures that stand nearest to the throne of God. The Seraphim appears in Christianity and Judaism. The singular "seraph" is a back-formation from the plural "seraphim", in Hebrew the singular is "Sarah."

Once I was working as a Medical Staff Coordinator in a hospital in Leesburg, Florida. I was being interviewed for the Director position of the hospital in West Palm Beach, Florida. I interviewed for well over an hour when the Director of Medical Affairs said something very strange to me. He said something that no interviewer has ever said. I was not expecting or prepared for his next question. He said, "Betsy, if you can tell me something I don't know I'll give you the job right now." I said a quick prayer under my breath, "God if this job is for me, give me what I need right now in the mighty name of Jesus."

I began to speak and had no idea as to what I was about to say. It was one of those times when my ears heard what my mouth was saying as it was being said. I asked, "How many wings do Seraphim have?" The doctor sat there in silence so long I thought he wasn't going to reply at all. Finally, he said, "I'm sorry, I don't know that."

I replied gleefully and said, "six, they have six wings according to Isaiah 6:2. **Isaiah 6:2... "Above Him stood the seraphim; each one had six wings, with twain he covered his face, and with twain he covered his feet, and with twain he did fly."** I was rejoicing in my heart and spirit not only for the job but because the Lord had given me what I needed in that moment in time when I needed it. The doctor said, "You are hired, when can you start?"

Sometimes it's not the big things that you need, such as with my job. Even the small things that are important to you are also important to God. Think about that for a moment. If it crosses your mind and you dwell on it, then it is important to the Lord also. I find great comfort in knowing the

Lord hears my thoughts and sees my heart and knows where I'm at all the times both spiritually and physically. I am never alone as He is always with me. **Deuteronomy 31:8 "The Lord himself goes before you and will be with you, he will never leave you nor forsake you (NIV)."**

The Secret of Psalm 91

Psalm 91 holds a secret. Most people read right through that and never see the secret. Let's look at it now... **Psalm 91, "He that dwelleth in the secret place of the most high shall abide under the shadow of the Almighty. I will say of the Lord, He is my refuge and my fortress, my God in Him will I trust. Surely He shall deliver thee from the snare of the fowler and from the noisome pestilence. He shall cover thee with His feathers and under his wings shalt thou trust; His truth shall be thy shield and buckler. Thou shalt not be afraid for the terror by night, nor for the arrow that flieth by day, Nor for the pestilence that walketh in darkness, nor for the destruction that wasteth at noonday. A thousand shall fall at thy side and ten thousand at thy right hand, but it shall not come nigh thee. Only with thine eyes shall thou behold and see the reward of the wicked. Because thou has made the Lord**

which is my refuge, even the most High, thy habitation. Then shall no evil befall thee, neither shall any plague come nigh thy dwelling. For He shall give his angels charge over thee, to keep thee in all thy ways. They shall bear thee up in their hands, lest thou dash thy foot against a stone. Thou shalt tread upon the lion and adder, the young lion and the dragon shalt thou trample under feet. Because he hath set His love upon me, therefore will I deliver him; I will set him on high, because he hath known my name. He shall call upon me and I will answer him. I will be with him in trouble; I will deliver him and honor him. With long life will I satisfy him and show him my salvation."

He said above He has set his love upon you if you are a Christian. Therefore He will deliver him and He will set him on high because he hath known my name. He shall call upon me and I will answer him. I will be with him in trouble and I will deliver him and honor him. With long life will I satisfy him and show him my salvation. What is it that lets you dwell in the secret hiding place? What is it that allows you all the protection from this chapter? What is it that allows you to know He will answer you when you're in trouble and He will deliver you and honor you and give you a long life? It is because you have known His name!!!!! These promises are not available to everybody. Just to the people who know His name. You must have a close walk with Christ and you must know the glory of His name. Just hearing His name or reading His name, is not the same as knowing it. You must know it and have a relationship with Him.

If you are walking down the street and you meet a stranger and you say hey buddy can you do me a favor? Most likely the stranger is going to just keep walking.

Why? He keeps walking because he does not know you. He doesn't know your name and he doesn't know anything about you. But if you are walking down the street and you see your friend you will most likely say "Hey Fred, can you do me a favor?" Fred will be willing to help you out. Why? Fred is willing to help because he knows you personally. He knows your name and he knows you are a good guy. It's the same reasoning behind knowing who Christ is and Christ knowing who you are.

I know we have talked a lot about building a relationship with Christ. I also want to point out there are so many benefits available to you by serving the Lord. One of those benefits is to know that the Lord goes before you in all battles. That means spiritual battles, physical battles, financial battles, emotional battles and every other battle you face. Look at KJV…

Exodus 14:14 "The Lord shall fight for you and ye shall hold your peace."

Again, this scripture supports the written fact that the Lord will fight for you. Then in **Exodus 15:26 "If thou will diligently hearken to the voice of the Lord thy God, and wilt do that which is right in His sight, and will give ear to His commandments and keep all his statutes, I will put none of these diseases upon thee...for I am the Lord that healeth thee."**

Do you see what just happened here? FIRST, the Lord says He will fight for you and then He says he will heal you....BUT ONLY if you diligently hearken to His voice. BUT ONLY, if you seek Him, build that relationship and ONLY if, you communicate with Him. Yes, life can be hard, very hard sometimes. You might be under attack but you are also under His blood. Isn't it worth it just to know that the Lord knows who you are and He knows where you are? He also knows what battles or mountains you are facing in your life and He will go ahead of you and fight for you. Then He will heal you. Why? If you go back to what we said earlier in **Psalm 91**....the answer is right there...Why? Because you have called upon his name! Because you have created a relationship with Him and because you have chosen to serve Him!

One evening I received a phone call from my daughter. She was telling me that I needed to come over to her house right away because something was going wrong, really wrong. We jumped in the car and headed over there. We were praying on the way and getting ready to face whatever battle was taking place.

We walked in the house and shut the door. Immediately there was a knock on the door that sounded more like a pounding noise. I started to walk to the door and my husband said, "Don't open that door!!" We stood in the living room and we could hear moaning sounds. We walked around the house and could not see anything out of place. So where was the moaning coming from? We continued to pray. We opened the anointing oil and began to anoint her house. We walked around and stopped in the living room. Her house had an upstairs balcony and the bedrooms were all upstairs. As we stood downstairs praying in a circle, the pillows from the bed began to fly over the railing off the balcony towards us below.

We went back upstairs and then we saw it…. There it was right in front of us…. My daughter had just returned from a cruise to the islands. She purchased two little dolls from the islands. Both of those dolls were dressed in colorful garb and looked like the island people. While they were cute and colorful they turned out to be Voodoo dolls. We kept praying and my husband took the dolls out of the house and put them in the barbeque grill. He then poured gas on them and set them on fire. My daughter and I were still inside the house praying. We could hear all kinds of horrible screams coming from the dolls outside as they were burning. After several minutes my husband opened the grill just to find out the Voodoo dolls had not burned. They were scorched around the edges but not burned. He put more gas on them and set them on fire again. And again...and again but they were not burning. It wasn't until we poured anointing oil and gas on them that they began to burn. We tied the lid shut on the grill. We loaded it in the trunk of the car and took it to the landfill and dug a hole and buried it.

When we talk about spiritual warfare, this is only one example. We face many things in life. It is of vital importance to be close to Christ and prayed up so you are ready for battle. Any time the phone rings it could be a call to battle, especially if you are called to be a prayer warrior. It could be a call from someone somewhere that needs you to be the powerful prayer warrior that we are called to be. It could be YOU who needs help or a touch from God. I always say, "God Bless the First Responders." This means the prayer warriors also. We need to be instant in season and out as the bible says. Second Timothy 4:2 tells us to "**preach the word, be instant in season, out of season; reprove, rebuke, exhort with all longsuffering and doctrine.**"

We need to exercise our faith. Strong faith allows us to speak words and the words we speak form images in the spirit and the spirit brings it to reality in our physical world.

Don't Sell Out

Once you make the decision, to serve the Lord, your life will change. Satan will now take more notice of you. He doesn't feel he has much to worry about when you are not saved. When you are not living a life for Christ, he has little worries. He is content with some people knowing the truth as long as they don't try to live the truth. A good example here would be the people who go to church every Sunday and sit in the same place and sing the same songs but have an empty heart. They don't serve Christ with all they have. They appear to be Christians but are in reality only churchgoers. They live in sin all week long but are still happy to go to church on Sunday, just for the show of it and just in case anyone should notice them.

There was a prideful lady once who went to church every Sunday. She sat near the front in the same spot every Sunday.

She wore fancy dresses and big hats. She was so proud of herself and wanted to be seen. One Sunday morning the preacher was speaking on the topic of getting in the way of Christ. She got so caught up in the phrase "get in the way", all of a sudden she jumped up to her feet and started yelling, "I'm in the way, I'm in the way!" At that moment a gentleman sitting behind her yelled out, "yes, Lady and maybe if you'd get out of the way somebody else could get in." Going to church is not all there is. We must be born again. We must confess our sins to Christ, ask Him to forgive us and ask Him to save us. We must have works that follow us. **James 2:20 "But wilt thou know, Oh vain man, that faith without works is dead?"**

Once we make the decision, to follow Christ we have faith to build, work to do and a kingdom to serve. We never look back to where we have been once we give our life to Christ. We never give in when satan attacks us and we never sell out. For joy cometh in the morning and our reward will be great if we endure the journey. You have to be aware of satan's evil tactics. He has a way of making his ideas look so great to you. He has a way of making the world look so inviting and glorious. When in fact, all he is trying to do is lead you down the wrong road in life.

It's like you are driving down the freeway and you pass exits. There are signs before you get to the exit. They tell you about gas stations and places to eat and they are just ahead. There may be signs with a picture of a big juicy steak and boy it looks good. You've been driving for a long time and you are tired and hungry. So you get off at the exit and you track down the steak house and after spending time and money which gets you off your schedule, you walk away saying "that was a dry, hard, piece of leather." Then you are sorry you ever left the highway.

That's the way it is with satan. He tries to tempt you and make you think you are getting something very good but it is deception. He is trying to make you believe you don't need the Lord. Why would you want the Lord? After all aren't you doing just fine without Him? The answer is NO! No, you are not doing fine without Him. You are not gaining any rewards here on earth unless you are serving Him and living for Him.

The point is satan will promise you anything to get total control over your life. He does not care about you. All he cares about is getting that total control so he can come in steal, kill and destroy. **John 10:10 "The thief cometh not, but for to steal, and to kill, and to destroy: I (Jesus) am come that they might have life, and that they**

might have *it* **more abundantly."** He is not after you...He is after your soul. He is the deceiver, he is a liar and he is the one who comes as your buddy, your friend and tries to tell you he is who you should serve, because he has things he can give you. That is called deception. In the end, you will find yourself on the exit ramp of life's highway feeling alone and lost. **2 Timothy 3:5 "Having the form of godliness, but denying the power thereof; from such turn away."**

I have a dear friend that I have known for years. She was faced with the offer of all her dreams to come true. Her name is Kimberlee Coleman Lightsey. She lives in central Florida and here is her story in her own words. I have not added anything or taken anything away from her story. **"My family began a Southern Gospel singing ministry called The Faith Family Singers in the late 1990's. We mainly focused on providing Sunday services to local nursing** home residents. As time progressed, we had the opportunity to open shows for some semi-professional groups. This led to us releasing our first album, "A Call of Faith." It wasn't long before the singing became more of a passion than a hobby. With bookings were becoming more frequent and the release of my first solo album, "Strong in the Spirit."

I realized that this would be something I would enjoy doing as a career. Like a good grandparent, my grandfather, Billy Yearly, set out to make my dream a reality. He had handed out my promo CD all over North and South Carolina. It finally made its way to Tennessee. His enthusiasm and persistence opened doors to auditions before some big-name promoters, including Eddie Crook of Daywind. My grandfather kept in touch through frequent phone calls updating me on the latest news. For some strange reason, none of these options felt like the "right fit" to me.

Then, at the age of 16, I will never forget the phone call I received late one evening while traveling. My grandpa could hardly contain his excitement. "Well girl, you'll never guess who I met today!" With a shake in his voice he went on to tell me that while in the teller line of a bank in Nashville, he was approached by a gentleman who noticed the promo CD in his arm. He asked, "Are you the grandpa of that Kimberlee Coleman girl?" To which he answered, "Of course!" Even though, he still wasn't sure of the identity of this man.

The stranger proceeded to tell my grandfather that he had heard my promo CD and was looking to sign one more star before he retired. He introduced himself and explained that he had helped produce such talent as Dolly Parton and Willie

Nelson. After giving out his contact information, he began to explain what he had envisioned for my future. "Bring her up here", he said, "and I will get her into vocal training. We will get her set up with a band and wardrobe. She will debut by opening for a big name star on a Saturday night on the Grand Ole Opry stage. I will do it all as long as she signs over total control to me."

I was in a state of shock when I hung up the phone. I mean, this is a moment many people only dream of getting to experience. My grandfather got slightly annoyed when I told him I needed to pray about it and would let him know my decision in a few days. The following few days were spent weighing the options and praying to see if this was the door God had opened for me. When the day finally came for me to give grandpa my answer, I didn't have a yes or a no from God. All I kept getting was a repeat of the gentleman saying, "I will do it all as long as she signs over total control." It was then I realized I had the answer the entire time.

A ministry MUST be led by God. Signing over "total control" to a man means I wouldn't be free to do or say what God would have me to. Since the beginning of my singing career, I've sung a song by Michael Combs titled, "Not for Sale." This was a real-life reflection of the part of that song that I had been singing for years. "I don't need popularity; I'd rather have what He gave to me!" Fame and fortune are not what God has called me into. He has given me a mission to share His love and the hope of salvation everywhere I go. I am a child of God and only He has "total control" of what happens to me. Temptations will arise but regardless of what the enemy dangles in front of you to cause you to sell out, just remember, Jesus paid it all!!!!" Say it with me "I'M NOT FOR SALE!"

(signed) In His Grip, Kimberlee Coleman Lightsey

Today Kimberlee and her family have a ministry in central Florida and she is living an extraordinary life. **Psalm 127:3-5 "Lo, children are an heritage of the Lord; and the fruit of the womb is his reward. As arrows are in the hand of a mighty man, so are children of the youth. Happy is the man that hath his quiver full of them; they shall not be ashamed, but they shall speak with the enemies in the gate."**

The question now would be...Do you know Him? Do you know His name? Have you asked Him to be your Lord and Savior? If you answered yes, that is great. There is always room to grow closer to him. If you answered no, you don't know Him; let me tell you, it is so easy. Just pray this simple prayer:

Lord, as I come to you today I'm asking forgiveness for all my sins and shortcomings. I want to be forgiven and saved so that I may truly know you and serve you. I surrender all that I am to you Lord, my creator and my Messiah, the Son of the Holy Father. Amen

If you prayed this short but sincere prayer the bible says you have taken the first big step to know who Christ is. Please find a good bible-based church and attend so that you may hear the word of God and grow. If you can't find a church contact us. We have prayer warriors in 30 states and 2 countries. We will help you find a place to grow. We also have a Facebook page: **Top of The World Conference**. Look us up and let us know if you have questions or need to leave a prayer request. Our website is: **Circleof7ministry.com**

Numbers 6:24-26 "The Lord bless you and keep you. The Lord make His face shine upon you and be gracious unto thee. The Lord lift up his countenance upon thee and give you peace."

The End

We are the called. We are the warriors. We are the first on the battlefield and the last ones off. Many divine miracles from God Himself are available to you.

Rev. Rosa Sikes and her family

www.ingramcontent.com/pod-product-compliance
Lightning Source LLC
Chambersburg PA
CBHW020118180726
47992CB00019B/750